13 Colonies

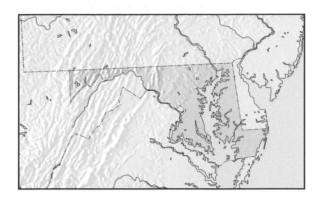

MARYLAND

13 Colonies

MARYLAND

THE HISTORY OF MARYLAND COLONY, 1634–1776

ROBERTA WIENER AND JAMES R. ARNOLD

Raintree
Chicago, Illinois

© 2005 Raintree
Published by Raintree,
A division of Reed Elsevier, Inc.
Chicago, IL

For information, address the publisher:
Raintree, 100 N. LaSalle, Suite 1200, Chicago, IL 60602

Printed and bound in China

08 07 06 05 04
10 9 8 7 6 5 4 3 2 1

Library of Congress Cataloging-in-Publication Data
Wiener, Roberta, 1952-
  Maryland / Roberta Wiener and James R. Arnold.
      p. cm. -- (13 colonies)
Summary: A detailed look at the formation of the colony of Maryland, its government, and its overall history, plus a prologue on world events in 1634 and an epilogue on Maryland today.
Includes bibliographical references and index.
  ISBN 0-7398-6880-2 (lib. bdg.) -- ISBN 1-4109-0304-4 (pbk.)
  1. Maryland--History--Colonial period, ca. 1600-1775--Juvenile literature. 2. Maryland--History--Revolution, 1775-1783--Juvenile literature. [1. Maryland--History--Colonial period, ca. 1600-1775. 2. Maryland--History--Revolution, 1775-1783.] I. Arnold, James R. II. Title. III. Series: Wiener, Roberta, 1952- 13 colonies.
  F184.W5 2004
  975.2'02--DC21
                        2003011057

Disclaimer

All the Internet addresses (URLs) given in this book were valid at the time of going to press. However, due to the dynamic nature of the Internet, some addresses may have changed, or sites may have changed or ceased to exist since publication. While the author and publishers regret any inconvenience this may cause readers, no responsibility for any such changes can be accepted by either the author or the publishers.

Some words are shown in bold, **like this.** You can find out what they mean by looking in the glossary.

Title page picture: Colonial shipbuilders

Opposite: A colonial settlement in northeastern Maryland, near the Pennsylvania border

The authors wish to thank Walter Kossmann, whose knowledge, patience, and ability to ask all the right questions have made this a better series.

Picture Acknowledgments

Architect of the Capitol: 57 bottom, 58-59 Colonial Williamsburg Foundation: 6 bottom, 7, 36, 48-49 top center, 49 top, 54 top ET Archives: 10 bottom J.G. Heck, Iconographic Encyclopedia of Science, Literature, and Art, 1851: 9 Independence National Historical Park: 56 bottom, 57 top Library of Congress: 6 top, 12, 13, 14, 15, 16-17, 20, 27, 39, 40-41, 45, 52, 54 bottom Maryland Historical Society, Baltimore, MD: 5, 29, 30-31, 32 top, 43, 44 top, 50, 53, 56 top National Archives: 8, 24, 32 bottom, 37, 38, 48 top, 49 center and bottom, 51, 55, 59 National Park Service, Colonial National Historical Park: Cover, title page, 17, 22-23, 34, 35, 44-45, 46-47, 48 bottom National Portrait Gallery, London, England: 10 top, 11

Contents

PROLOGUE: THE WORLD IN 1634

In 1634, the year the English arrived in Maryland, English colonists had already settled in Virginia, Massachusetts, New Hampshire, and Connecticut. Some Europeans had come to North America for riches, and others for the freedom to practice their chosen religion. Many, including the first English settlers of Maryland, came for both.

Europe had begun to explore the wider world during the Renaissance, a 150-year period of invention and discovery. Advances in navigation and the building of larger and better sailing ships allowed longer voyages. It was the

Above: In 1634 a person could still be arrested for arguing that Earth revolved around the Sun. Only in 1543 had the Polish scientist, Nicolaus Copernicus, published his daring idea that Earth was not the center of the universe. The famous astronomer and mathematician, Galileo, spent from 1634 until his death in 1642 under arrest for teaching people about the solar system.

Below: Europeans knew little about Africa, but they knew enough to see great opportunity. They saw the chance to grow rich from trade in exotic spices. They saw souls ready to be converted to Christianity. They also saw the chance to make conquests of their own and expand their countries into great empires. And not least, they saw the dark-skinned people of Africa and, considerng them a different species, they saw the chance to capture slaves. Below is a drawing of a slave traders' post on the coast of Africa.

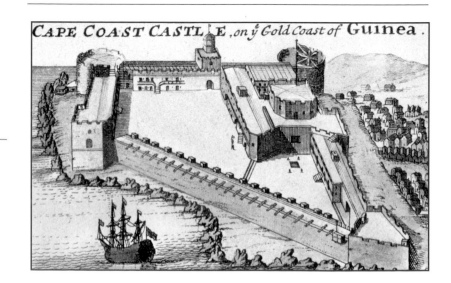

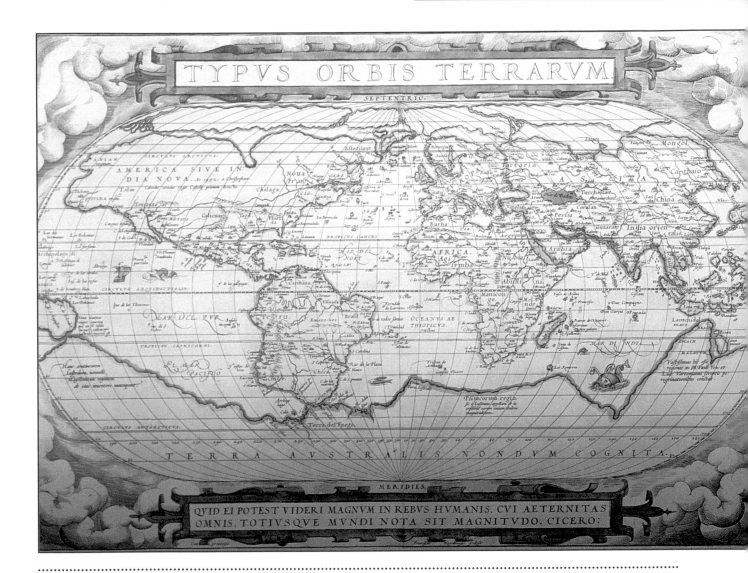

A map shows the world as seen by Europeans around 1570. During the age of exploration, a flock of birds flying from Europe, eastward over Asia, would first have seen the Turks, who had conquered a huge empire that encompassed much of Eastern Europe, the Middle East, and North Africa. This flock would then have seen that the Russians had just conquered and annexed Siberia. Flying east, the flock would come to China. Here was a land of some 60 million people, long ruled from Beijing by the Ming Dynasty. China was in decline but still looking for opportunities to conquer and expand. Conflict raged along China's borders, particularly with the Koreans and the Japanese. Continuing east, the flock would have crossed the water to Japan. Japan was recently unified under a single conqueror and had begun trading with Europeans for the first time. Had the flock then turned aroundover the Pacific Ocean and flown back west, they would have seen India.India was a great land of 100 million people, united by the conqueror, Akbar the Great. There stood the newly built Taj Mahal, a monument that remains one of the wonders of the world. Turning to the southwest, they would have found Africa. On the African coasts were small kingdoms and several great empires, often at war and often changing leadership. The interior of Africa remained unknown to outsiders.

NEW WORLD: WESTERN HEMISPHERE OF THE EARTH, INCLUDING NORTH AMERICA, CENTRAL AMERICA, AND SOUTH AMERICA; SO CALLED BECAUSE THE PEOPLE OF THE OLD WORLD, IN THE EAST, DID NOT KNOW ABOUT THE EXISTENCE OF THE AMERICAS UNTIL THE 1400S

Columbus and his sailors crossed the Atlantic Ocean in 1492.

Age of Exploration, with great seamen from Portugal, Spain, Italy, France, and England sailing into uncharted waters. Beginning in the 1400s, they reached Africa, India, the Pacific Ocean, China, Japan, and Australia. They encountered kingdoms and civilizations that had existed for centuries.

The voyages from Europe to these distant shores went around Africa. This made the trip long and dangerous. So, European explorers began to sail westward in search of shortcuts. On one such voyage, in 1492, Christopher Columbus landed on an island on the far side of the Atlantic Ocean and claimed it for Spain. He thought that he had actually sailed all the way around the world and come to an island near India. Ten more years of exploration by numerous sailors passed before the people of Europe realized that Columbus had been the first European of their era to set foot in a land unknown to them. They called this land the **New World**, although it was not new to the people who lived there. After Columbus, Amerigo Vespucci claimed to have reached the New World. Whether he actually did or not, a mapmaker put his name on a map in 1507, and the New World became America, or the Americas. Still looking for that

CATHOLIC: ROMAN CATHOLIC; THE OLDEST CHRISTIAN CHURCH ORGANIZATION, GOVERNED BY A HIERARCHY BASED IN ROME AND LED BY THE POPE.

PROTESTANT: ANY CHRISTIAN CHURCH THAT HAS BROKEN FROM AWAY FROM ROMAN CATHOLIC OR EASTERN ORTHODOX CONTROL

COLONY: LAND OWNED AND CONTROLLED BY A DISTANT NATION; A COLONIST IS A PERMANENT SETTLER OF A COLONY

The Spanish Inquisition, a court of powerful officials who answered only to King Ferdinand and Queen Isabella, used torture to get Jewish people to confess to the "crime" of heresy, belief in a religion other than Christianity. The Spanish executed thousands of Jews and Muslims in hideous public spectacles and forced about 170,000 to flee the country. Other Europeans, even while fighting their own religious wars, still viewed the extremes of the Spanish Inquisition with disgust.

shortcut to the riches of Asia, European explorers continued to sail to North and South America. They began to claim large pieces of these lands for their own nations.

By the time the first English people settled in Maryland, the French, mainly Roman **Catholics**, had founded three settlements in Canada, at Quebec, Trois Rivieres (near Quebec), and Acadia (also known as Nova Scotia). Far to the south, French **Protestants** had tried to start a **colony** in Florida. But the Spanish were far ahead of other Europeans in the competition for land in the Americas. Before the English came to America, the Spanish had already claimed huge portions of both North and South America. They had conquered two mighty Native American empires, and introduced the first domestic cattle and horses to the Americas. They founded the first two permanent cities—St. Augustine and Santa Fe —in what would become the United States. They had brought European civilization as well, including printing presses and universities. The Spanish also brought their chosen form of Christianity, Roman Catholicism, and converted hundreds of Native Americans, often by force.

Europe was no stranger to religious violence and intolerance when English people began looking for a

religious haven in America. Christians had long been going to war with Muslims and persecuting Jewish people. During the 1490s the Spanish and the Portuguese had expelled from their countries all Jews who refused to convert. European Christians had fought many wars, called Crusades, in the effort to drive Muslims from the Middle East and Europe. The Christian people of Europe and Britain also fought one another, in long and bloody religious wars.

For centuries in western Europe, Christianity and Roman Catholicism had been one and the same, with all Christians ruled from Rome by the Pope. But in 1517 Martin Luther, a German monk, protested some of the actions of the Roman Catholic church, and so began the Protestant Reformation.

In 1534 the English King Henry VIII took advantage of the Protestant Reformation. The Pope would not grant him a divorce, so he formed the Church of England and declared himself its head. The Church of England, also

called the **Anglican** church, became a Protestant church, independent of the Pope, but still Christian.

Then, in 1554, Queen Mary restored Catholicism as the official religion of England. She executed more than 250 people who had continued practicing Protestantism, and for this reason, people called her "Bloody Mary." Five years later, Queen Elizabeth I restored the Church of England. Under her rule, and that of the next two kings, Catholicism was outlawed, and those who continued to practice it faced arrest. A plot by a Catholic, Guy Fawkes, to blow up **Parliament** and kill the king in 1605 fanned the flames of Protestant distrust of Catholics in England. Meanwhile, in 1562, French Catholics and Protestants began fighting a series of bloody Wars of Religion, which lasted for more than 35 years. In 1566 Protestants in the Netherlands revolted against Catholic rule.

Even under Protestant rule, many English Protestants grew dissatisfied and formed churches to practice their own versions of Christianity. Among them were the **Pilgrims,** the Puritans, and the Quakers, all of whom suffered persecution for their beliefs and eventually chose to come to America. However, migration to America did not guarantee religious freedom to all. In the American colonies, Christian groups continued to **persecute** both one another and non-Christians. Only when the United States passed the Bill of Rights in 1791 did religious freedom and tolerance become the law of the land.

Opposite, Top: King Henry VIII cast off the authority of the Pope and opened the way for the Church of England to become a Protestant church.

Opposite, Bottom: A woman preaches at a Quaker meeting, an example of one way that new forms of Christianity differed from the Church of England.

PERSECUTE: TO PUNISH PEOPLE BECAUSE OF THEIR BELIEFS, RELIGION, OR RACE

Queen Elizabeth I restored the Church of England as the official religion of the country.

I.
THE LORDS BALTIMORE

Under English law, a Catholic could be fined for not attending the Church of England. This law was rarely enforced, and many Catholics enjoyed privileged and prosperous lives in England. George Calvert, the first Lord Baltimore, had such a privileged life. He graduated from college and traveled in Europe before settling down to a career in government service. However, in 1625, Calvert publicly admitted his Catholicism and resigned as England's secretary of state. Calvert did this in part because his son, Cecilius, was married to a Catholic, Anne Arundell, the daughter of his friend Sir Thomas Arundell. However, Calvert remained on good terms with the king, and his resignation did not interfere with his longstanding interest in expanding his family's land holdings in the American colonies.

Calvert had bought stock in the Virginia Company, joined the council of the New England Company, and bought part of the Avalon Peninsula in Newfoundland. Avalon became the site of a colony in 1620. Calvert first visited this colony in the summer and decided to settle there with his family, but their first cold winter at Avalon changed their minds. Calvert sent his children back to England and sailed with his wife to Virginia in 1628. The Virginia colonists, loyal members of the Church of England, would not let the Calverts leave their ship unless they took an oath renouncing Catholicism. They refused.

So Calvert returned to England and asked King Charles I for land on which to found a colony as a haven for Catholics. At this time there were about 55,000 Catholics living in England. In 1632 the king granted Calvert about 12 million acres of land around the Chesapeake Bay, land that had once belonged to the disbanded Virginia Company. George Calvert died in April 1632, and his 26-year-old son, Cecilius, inherited the grant. Two months later, Cecilius received a **charter** to settle the land. The land was called Maryland, after the king's Catholic wife, Henrietta Maria.

George Calvert graduated from Oxford, traveled around Europe, and learned three foreign languages. He held several high government posts, including that of England's secretary of state. Calvert was knighted by King James I, and so could call himself Sir George Calvert. After Calvert resigned from the government, King Charles I gave him the title of Lord Baltimore. The first Lord Baltimore lived to be 52 years old.

CHARTER: DOCUMENT CONTAINING THE RULES FOR RUNNING AN ORGANIZATION

Who Was Lord Baltimore?

In England a person of high social standing can have a title, which makes him a member of the nobility. The nobility is a step below royalty, the word that describes the king and queen and their families. Lord, lady, sir, dame, baron, and baroness are examples of titles that members of the nobility can use with their names. Titles can be inherited or granted by the king. Some titled people also own a large estate and use the title with the name of the estate instead of with their names.

Sir George Calvert was England's secretary of state under King James I. He had received the title Lord Baltimore, along with a great estate in Ireland, from King Charles I. Such titles and estates are passed from father to eldest son. Younger sons do not get the title. So a younger brother of any Lord Baltimore simply used his family name, Calvert.

The first Lord Baltimore died in 1632. The title passed to his eldest son, Cecilius, who became the second Lord Baltimore, and the first Lord Proprietor of the Maryland colony. The younger brother of Cecilius, Leonard Calvert, became the first governor of the Maryland colony and held that office for about 12 years. The second Lord Baltimore died in 1675, and the title passed to his son, Charles Calvert.

Cecilius Calvert. Each colony, regardless of type, had a governor, an appointed council (similar to the upper house of a legislature, such as the House of Lords in England's Parliament), plus an elected lower house. The lower house had different names in different colonies. In Virginia it was called the House of Burgesses, in Maryland, the House of Delegates, or the Assembly. Cecilius Calvert's brother and two sons each served as colonial governor of Maryland.

Before Charles Calvert became the third Lord Baltimore, he also served as Maryland's governor from 1662 to 1675. He lived until 1714, but lost the colony when Maryland Protestants rebelled in 1689. His son, Benedict Calvert, became the fourth Lord Baltimore, and regained Maryland because he had converted to the Church of England. However, he lived barely a year after his father's death, so his young son, also named Charles Calvert, became the fifth Lord Baltimore. Calvert's guardian had to serve in his place as Lord Proprietor of Maryland until the boy reached adulthood. The fifth Lord Baltimore lived until 1751, but visited the colony only once, in 1732. The town of Baltimore was named for him.

Frederick Calvert, the sixth and last Lord Baltimore, paid little attention to the colony during his 20 years as Lord Proprietor, and died in 1771 without leaving a legal heir to the title. All of the Calverts who held the title and ruled Maryland are sometimes referred to as a group, the "Lords Baltimore" or the "Lords Proprietor."

JESUIT: MEMBER OF THE SOCIETY OF JESUS, A MEN'S RELIGIOUS ORDER FOUNDED IN 1540. JESUITS HAVE ALWAYS BEEN VERY ACTIVE AS MISSIONARIES AROUND THE WORLD.

King Charles I and his French Catholic wife, Henrietta Maria. The American colonies had different types of charters. Maryland's charter was proprietary, meaning the king granted the land to a private owner, Lord Baltimore and his heirs. When Maryland was later changed to a royal colony, the king took a more direct role in the colonial government by choosing the governor and making the laws.

The charter gave Cecilius Calvert an unusual amount of power over his colony. As the colony's proprietor, he had absolute power over the government and defense of Maryland, and could distribute land to whomever he wished without first getting the king's approval. Still, Calvert had to distribute some of the land fairly or he would be unable to attract settlers. He offered generous land grants to all settlers. Every free adult received 100 acres and every child 50. They paid a very small yearly rent for the land, less than half an English **pound** for 100 acres. Wealthy men who invested in the colony received much larger grants of a thousand acres or more. Calvert had to spend a large sum of his own money to get the colony started, paying for shipping and supplies as well as advertising and promoting the colony. The **Jesuits,** a Catholic order, also helped finance the new colony.

In addition to offering land, Calvert also sought to attract settlers by promising to tolerate non-Catholics. His decision attracted numerous Puritans and Quakers who were fleeing the religious intolerance of Virginia. It proved to be a particularly wise decision because these people had colonial experience in Virginia. This experience helped the new colony succeed. Calvert decided that both Catholics and Protestants could participate in government, and that they could freely practice their chosen religions. However, he made it illegal for Catholics to try to convert Protestants or for Protestants to convert Catholics. Nor could they argue about religion in public. Calvert expected both groups to co-exist in peace.

Wealthy Virginians protested Calvert's charter. As Calvert advertised for Catholic colonists to sail in 1633, Virginians worked to stop him. Supporters of Virginia even tried to hire away his sailors. They succeeded in delaying the Maryland colonists by getting the Privy Council (the king's closest advisors) to insist on an oath of allegiance from all settlers before they set sail from London. This oath required all takers to deny the Pope as their religious leader. Some colonists avoided taking the oath by hiding from authorities. Others boarded the ships after they left London. So, in spite of many obstacles, Calvert managed to recruit colonists to settle in Maryland.

2.
ATLANTIC CROSSING

Lord Baltimore stayed in London to defend his charter from opponents. He sent his younger brother, Leonard Calvert, to govern the new colony. Leonard Calvert took charge of some 150 people on two ships, the Ark and the Dove, which finally left England in November 1633. This group included seventeen Catholic gentlemen who were investors in the colony, the Calvert household, Jesuit priests, and mainly Protestant **indentured** servants. Only a few women accompanied them, and no children. Many more people had been interested in going, but had been discouraged by the obstacles put in their path by the colony's opponents.

> INDENTURE: AGREEMENT TO WORK FOR SOMEONE FOR A CERTAIN NUMBER OF YEARS, IN EXCHANGE FOR FOOD, A PLACE TO SLEEP, AND PAYMENT OF ONE'S PASSAGE ACROSS THE ATLANTIC TO THE COLONIES

The ships encountered two violent storms and became separated. Each feared the other had been lost at sea as they made the seven-week Atlantic crossing without one another's company and protection. The two ships found each other in a port in the West Indies, on the island of Barbados. Most of the passengers had survived long weeks of cramped conditions and poor food, living in a single small space below deck, surrounded by a year's worth of food and supplies. The colonists lingered for several weeks on Barbados, where the resident English **planters** took them in. They recovered from their voyage, enjoying fresh food and the warm climate. Finally they pushed off from Barbados for the three-week voyage up the coast to Maryland.

Father Andrew White offers a prayer of thanks for the first colonists' safe arrival in Maryland.

The colonists arrived at an island in the Potomac River in March 1634. On March 25, 1634, the priests offered a mass of thanksgiving, the first mass said within

Below: "The Indians began to lose fear and come … sometimes aboard our ship, wondering where that tree should grow, out of which so great a canoe should be hewn, supposing it all of one piece, as their canoes used to be."

the new colony of Maryland. This day is still celebrated as Maryland Day. The new arrivals had every reason to be thankful.

The arrival of the two English ships, monstrously large to Native American eyes, alarmed the Yaocomico people who lived along the Potomac. They lit great signal fires along the riverbanks to warn their people of the strange arrivals. The colonists at first feared the Native Americans would attack. However, Calvert, with the help of a Virginia fur trader who acted as interpreter, met with the chief and found him agreeable. The chief gave the colonists permission to settle on his land, and in fact welcomed an English settlement as protection against hostile tribes from the north.

Below: Father White wrote of the colonists' dealings with the first Native Americans they saw, "To avoid all occasion of dislike, and color of wrong, we bought the space of thirty miles of ground [from] them, for axes, hoes, cloth, and hatchets."

3.
MARYLAND IN 1634

Before Europeans came to North America, trees covered most of the land. The trees grew so densely that it was said a squirrel could travel from the Atlantic coastline to the Mississippi River without having to touch the ground. Modern scientists call these trees the Eastern Deciduous Forest. (Deciduous means that the tree sheds it leaves in the autumn and grows new ones in the spring.) The two most common types of trees in the Eastern Deciduous Forest of the 17th century were oak and hickory.

When Europeans first arrived, trees covered about 90 percent of Maryland. The old, or mature, forests had little underbrush. The Englishman, John Smith, who had explored and mapped the Chesapeake Bay and part of the Potomac River in 1608, wrote that "a man may gallop a horse amongst these woods" in any direction. Streams meandered through the dark forests and provided splendid habitats for beavers. The beavers built dams across the streams to make ponds. These ponds offered special habitats for many kinds of wildlife. When old trees died, they fell into the streams to create a maze of logs, limbs, and roots that sheltered fish and other aquatic animals. Rain soaked into the forest floor and then seeped slowly into the streams. This process gave the streams fresh water even during dry periods.

The arrival of the Europeans changed the forests and the streams. The first settlers cut trees to provide fuel for fires and to clear land for farming and houses. They cleared and dug out stream channels to make way for boats, and filled in wetlands to make more farmland. As time passed, there were no more trees along the streams and rivers. Without trees to provide shade, the streams became warmer and this changed what could live in the water. Before, the trees trapped the soil. With the trees gone, the soil washed into the streams and rivers making them muddier and less able to support aquatic life.

There were no longer fallen trees to block the streams, so nutrients, chemicals naturally created when vegetable matter decays, swept downstream into the Chesapeake

Bay. This process began a set of changes that continues into present times.

The land that became the Maryland Colony includes three regions. The Coastal Plain lies along the Atlantic Ocean and extends inland to the **fall line,** or the place where the rivers fall rapidly from higher ground onto the flatter plain. The Coastal Plain covers about half of Maryland. In the middle of Maryland is the Piedmont, an area of rolling hills. To the west is the Appalachian Plateau, made up of the Blue Ridge, Valley and Ridge, and Allegheny Plateau. Here lies Maryland's share of the Appalachian Mountains, including its highest point, Backbone Mountain, at 3,360 feet (1,024 meters). There are eighteen large river basins in Maryland, the largest of which is formed by the Potomac River, which forms Maryland's southern boundary separating it from Virginia.

The climate depends on elevation and closeness to the Atlantic Ocean and the Chesapeake Bay. The coastal plain is usually hot and humid in the summer with temperatures sometimes over 100°F. (37°C.). In the winter the

FALL LINE: THE POINT AT WHICH A RIVER BEGINS FLOWING FROM HIGH GROUND TOWARD SEA LEVEL

Maryland geography

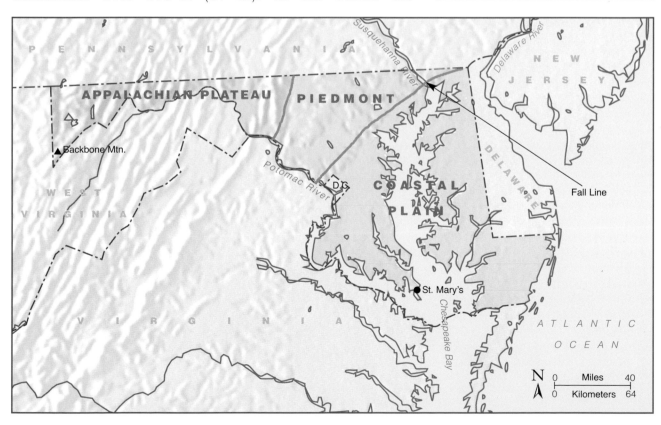

Like the Native Americans farther to the south in Virginia, the Inative peoples in the Maryland part of the Chesapeake Bay built bark-covered huts and had stockades around their villages to defend against attack by tribes from the north. Wrote Father White, "... they had wars with the [Susquehannocks], who come sometimes upon them, and waste and spoil them and their country ...."

temperature seldom falls as low as 15°F (−9°C) and more often stays around 40°F (4°C). These temperatures provide an eight-month-long growing season. Farther west, summers are almost as hot and winters are much colder. Everywhere there is usually ample rain to support the growing of food crops.

The Chesapeake Bay is Maryland's most important natural feature. It was here that Europeans first encountered Native Americans, who had lived in eastern North America for thousands of years. The native peoples lived in permanent villages. Near their homes they prepared large fields for farming. Women did most of the farmwork. They made small mounds within these fields in which they planted corn along with squash and beans. Together, these crops provided a stable food base. The Native Americans built storage places, either above or below ground, to preserve their food from one harvest until the next. They used wild foods, such as nuts and berries, to supplement what they grew.

Maryland was rich with wildlife. The Chesapeake Bay had tremendous numbers of fin fish and shellfish. Native Americans living near the water caught and ate fish, blue crabs, oysters, and clams. Huge populations of waterfowl such as ducks and geese lived in the coastal marshes. An Englishman wrote in 1635 that there were "Whales, Sturgeons, very large and good, and in great abundance, Grampuses, Porpuses, Mullets, Trouts, Soules, Place, Mackerell, Perch, Crabs, Oysters, Cockles, and Mussles" and many other fish that had no English name. The inland forests gave food and shelter to large populations of wild animals. Many were useful to humans. The most important food animals, deer and wild turkey, were plentiful. Otters, beavers, and minks provided valuable fur. Timber wolves, bears, cougars, and bobcats roamed through the forests hunting for prey.

In 1600 about 2,700 Native Americanss lived along Maryland's Eastern Shore (the area of Maryland bordered on the east by the Atlantic Ocean and on the west by the Chesapeake Bay). The most numerous were the Nanticokes, a group with about 1,600 people who belonged to the Algonquian linguistic (language) family. Along the southern part of the Eastern Shore lived the Accohanocs. They were part of the Powhatans, the people who occupied the land where the first Englishmen settled in Virginia. The Conoys lived on the western side of the Chesapeake Bay. They were related to the Powhatans and Nanticokes. Farther west, the Shawnees, a warrior people, lived in the Maryland mountains as well as along the Susquehanna River.

The group who had the greatest impact upon the first colonists were the Susquehannocks. The Susquehannock belonged to the Iroquoian linguistic family. They lived on the Susquehanna River in what was to become New York and Pennsylvania as well as Maryland. When Europeans first encountered the Susquehannocks, the Susquehannocks were at war with the Iroquois. The Iroquois put pressure on the northern boundary of the Susquehannocks, and the Susquehannocks, in turn, put pressure on Native Americans living farther south, including the Conoy people. It was Susquehannock pressure that forced the Yaocomicos, who lived along the bay, to agree readily to abandon their village at what was to become St. Mary's, allowing the first Englishmen to live there.

The arrival of the Europeans changed the ecological balance. The colonists brought with them animals and plants that were new to North America. Some of these they brought on purpose: horses, sheep, honeybees, wheat, and grapevines. As early as 1635 an Englishman noted that settlers had brought from Virginia "Hogges, Poultrey, and some Cowes ... which hath given them a foundation for breed and increase." The settlers built fences around their

Maryland First Impressions

One of the first settlers, the Jesuit priest Father Andrew White, wrote a detailed account of the first English settlement in Maryland. He commented favorably on almost all that he saw.

The land:
"The soil ... is so excellent that we cannot set down a foot, but tread on Strawberries, ... fallen mulberry vines, acorns, walnuts. ... All is high woods except where the Indians have cleared for corn. It abounds with delicate springs which are our best drink. ... The place abounds not alone with profit, but also with pleasure."

The Potomac River:
"This is the sweetest and greatest river I have seen. ..."

The inhabitants:
Father White described how the Indians came "... running to us with smiling countenance, and will help us in fishing, fowling, hunting, or what we please."

He was impressed with the Native Americans' friendliness and intelligence. In his eyes, religion was the only thing they lacked: "If these were ... Christian, they would doubtless be a virtuous and renowned nation. They exceedingly desire civil life and Christian apparel. ..."

A 1635 pamphlet published in England reported, "This Country affords naturally, many excellent things for Physicke and Surgery, the perfect use of which, the English cannot yet learn from the Natives." The English settlers soon learned from the Native Americans how to find the plants that had medicinal uses.

property and let their livestock run free outside the fences: "The Hogs run where they want and find their own Support in the Woods without any Care of the Owners." The hogs reproduced and formed populations of wild, or feral, animals. And this too changed the environment.

The settlers also accidentally brought some living things to America, including rats and weeds. When the new species came in contact with native species, some of the new species changed the environment. For example, the weeds brought by accident grew rapidly and spread quickly. Weeds like dandelions and thistles were able to out-compete the native plants. All of them grew well around cleared land. So when a colonist cleared land for his home and to plant crops, he created a place where native plants could not live and European weeds grew happily. When native plants died off, wildlife that depended on these plants either moved away or also died.

"When land is tired of tobacco, it will bear Indian corn or English wheat … with wonderful increase." Clearing land with hand tools was extremely hard work. Early colonial fields were not nearly this big.

But the biggest changes came from rats and from new diseases. The European rats were larger and more aggressive than the native rats. They escaped from the colonists' ships onto the land. They reproduced quickly and spread inland where they destroyed crops and, more importantly, ate the food that the Native Americans had stored to feed themselves through the winter.

The Europeans also accidentally brought new diseases to Maryland. The most common were smallpox, measles, chicken pox, scarlet fever, typhus, influenza, whooping cough, diphtheria, and bubonic plague. These diseases had attacked Europeans for one generation after another. Over time, Europeans had developed some immunity to the diseases. But the native peoples had never encountered these diseases and had no immunity. The diseases killed the Native Americans in large numbers. For example, the number of Conoys fell from 2,000 in 1600 to about 150 by 1765.

4.
IN THE BEGINNING

The first English settlement lay in the southern part of the land granted to the Calvert family. There the Yaocomicos had built a village overlooking a river that fed into the Potomac River. They were a peaceful farming people who had been the target of raids by Susquehannocks. The Yaocomicos had already decided to abandon their village to escape from the Susquehannocks, when the Ark and Dove arrived. So Calvert traded hatchets, hoes, and cloth for the Native Americans' village and 30 miles (48 kilometers) of surrounding land. He allowed the native people to remain there long enough to harvest their crops. The colonists landed, renamed the village St. Mary's, and made it their capital. Their first task was to build a **stockade** around the village to protect themselves against a possible attack.

STOCKADE: SERIES OF WOODEN POSTS SET INTO THE GROUND, FORMING A HIGH WALL TO PROTECT A SETTLEMENT

Maryland's first settlers built a stockade for protection from Native Americans, but soon decided they didn't have to live inside it.

Because beaver fur was so valuable, settlers trapped beavers until almost none survived in Maryland. Native Americans traded beaver pelts for the items they most wanted from the English: cloth, metal tools, and guns and gunpowder. At first the Maryland colonial government tried to prevent the Native Americans from acquiring guns, so the Native Americans traded instead with the Dutch and Swedish to the north because they had no such restrictions. Maryland had to offer guns if they wanted to receive furs.

The founders of the Maryland colony were determined to learn from the experiences of the Virginia Company's settlers 25 years earlier. They planned to arrive in early spring so they would have time to plant their crops and avoid a winter of starvation. They wanted also to grow rich as **planters**. The Calverts hoped their investors would prosper quickly in the fur trade, then establish large estates and grow cash crops for export.

The new colonists, having arrived in spring as planned, first planted corn to feed their animals and other food crops to feed themselves. They were able to use fields of rich soil that had already been cleared by Native Americans. They lived on the supplies they had brought and the abundant wild game while waiting for the harvest.

The first harvest was plentiful, but the fur trade turned out to be a disappointment. The colonists obtained very few furs, and many of them rotted while the Dove underwent repairs before returning to England. The final blow to hopes for an early profit from fur trading came when the Dove was lost at sea with its small cargo of furs.

Although Calvert had planned on the colonists living together in a town for protection, it proved unnecessary. The colonists had paid the Native Americans for the land and made an effort to get along with them. The local Native Americans remained peaceful, and the colonists soon moved away from the fort. They preferred to live apart from one another, each on his own plantation.

Calvert had also planned for his wealthy investors to grow even richer by establishing great estates. But this, too, did not turn out as planned. The gentlemen did not have enough servants to make huge plantations pay. As soon as the servants gained their free-

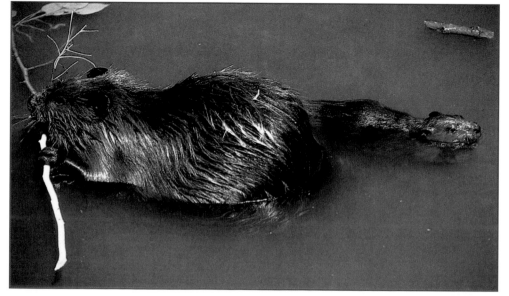

William Claiborne, a Virginian who had been trading for furs with the Native Americans in Maryland, did not welcome the arrival of the Maryland colonists and became a bitter enemy.

dom, they moved away to their own land and worked only for themselves. Maryland colony had plenty of cheap land but not enough laborers to work on it. Calvert had expected to duplicate the rigid English class system in Maryland, but instead, Maryland provided a chance for servants to improve their lives. As a result, small plantations soon outnumbered large ones in Maryland. Of male servants who arrived during Maryland colony's first ten years, nine out of ten became landowners, and many of them came to hold political offices and positions of leadership.

The Maryland colonists suffered some of the same hardships endured by the Virginians. In Maryland the settlers died of malaria, spread by mosquitos, and other deadly diseases caused by tainted water. Like the Virginia colonists, early Maryland colonists could expect to live only to their mid-40s. Maryland's English population grew slowly, as at least one settler in five sickened and died. During the first twenty years, men outnumbered women four to one. Few marriages were made or children born. Ten years after the first English settlers arrived in Maryland, the English population was still under 400. Another 15 years passed before the English population climbed to about 2,500.

Indentured Servants and Transported Criminals

To survive and prosper in the colonies required long hours of labor. Indentured servitude solved the problems of both master and servant. The master needed servants and the work they could do, and poor English people needed a way to pay for the voyage across the Atlantic. Indentured servitude was based on a deal between two people. A colonist paid the ocean passage of a person in exchange for four to seven years of work. So anxious were some to try their luck in the New World that they were willing to sell themselves into servitude, a form of slavery, to get there.

Businessmen recruited servants in England and then sold their indentures, or contracts, to settlers when they arrived in the colonies. The average age of a male servant on arrival in Maryland was 17. During their contracts, servants received only food, clothing, and shelter. On earning their freedom, they were supposed to receive from their masters food, clothing, and tools with which to make a fresh start. In addition, freed male servants received 50 acres of land. Fewer than one in five servants was female. Male servants were in greater demand to work in the fields. Also, without the promise of eventual landownership, servitude was less appealing to women.

Between 1718 and 1775, half of all arriving English colonists, about 50,000 in all, were convicted criminals, sentenced to transportation to the colonies. Four out of five of them were sent to Maryland and Virginia, usually on tobacco trading ships. Maryland alone received more than 9,000 of the convicts between 1748 and 1755. Many died of malnutrition or jail fever (another name for typhus, a disease spread by fleas). Their term of servitude was usually 14 years, twice that of the non-criminal indentured servant. Their purchase price was about a third of the price of a male African slave. They were treated like slaves, often working as field hands on smaller tobacco plantations. They received no land on completion of their terms and did not enjoy the same social status as freed indentured servants.

Even when an indentured servant survived his term and gained his freedom, he faced a difficult path from servant to landowner. He first had to work as a tenant farmer on someone else's land in order to make some money. He needed money to have his land grant surveyed, register his deed of ownership, clear the land, build a house, and survive until he harvested his first crops.

Tobacco could be grown successfully in many places along the Atlantic coast. What made Maryland special was the many streams and rivers that flowed into the Chesapeake Bay. These water highways offered a convenient way to move tobacco and other goods between farms and ships. The first colonists spread out from St. Mary's to live along Maryland's waterways, moving inland along navigable rivers. As long as they settled below the fall line they could

THIS INDENTURE Witnesseth, That *Casper Baur hath Bound & put his Three Children ye William Baur George Baur & Henry Baur Servants to Capt Charles Ridgely*

for and in Consideration of the Sum of *Twenty Three pounds Eighteen Shillings Currant Money* — paid by *Capt Charles Ridgely ye* for the Freight and other Charges *of his said three Children* in the Ship *Brittania Captdenott* from *Rotterdam* to *Maryland*, as also for other good Causes, *I* the said *Casper Baur* hath bound and put *his ye Three Children* and by these Presents doth bind and put *them* Servant to the said *Charles Ridgely* to serve *him his* Executors, and Assigns from the Day of the Date hereof, for and during the full Term of *their annual at Age of twenty* from thence next ensuing. During all which Term, the said Servant *his said Master his* Executors or Assigns, faithfully shall serve, and that honestly and obediently in all Things, as a good and dutiful Servant ought to do. AND the said *Charles Ridgely his* Executors and Assigns, during the said Term, shall find and provide for the said Servant, sufficient Meat, Drink, *Apparrell* Washing and Lodging, *And at the Expiration of their servitude to give them the Customary freedom Dues — William Baur being six years Old the Eleventh Day of Septembr Last George Baur being four years Old the Seventh Day of November Next, & Henry Baur being two years Old the Ninth day of May Next*

AND for the true Performance hereof, both the said Parties bind themselves firmly unto each other by these Presents. *In Witness whereof* they have hereunto interchangeably set their Hands and Seals. Dated the *Twenty Sixth* Day of *October* in the Fifth Year of his Majesty's Reign, Annoque Domini, 17*65*

Sealed and Delivered in Presence of us,

Johann Caspar Bauer

A 1765 indenture agreement. A father arranged for the servitude of his three children, aged 2, 4, and 6, until they reached the age of 21. Their master paid the children's passage across the Atlantic. Many parents considered such a long term of service to be a fair price to pay for their children to have a chance at the opportunities offered by a new land.

Daniel Dulany the Elder came from Ireland to Maryland in the early 1700s as an indentured servant. A lawyer who needed a clerk paid his passage. By the time Dulany had served out his indenture, he had learned enough to qualify as a lawyer. He married his employer's daughter and became wealthy and prominent, holding several political offices. His son, Daniel Dulany the Younger, attended the best schools in England, married an heiress, and became one of the biggest landowners in Maryland.

remain in contact with the ocean. For this reason, wealthy planters carved plantations out of the forest, on the large tracts of choice riverfront land granted them by the proprietor. They built their own docks so they could ship the plantation's tobacco and receive goods from England.

Maryland's early planters had no need for ports or towns. By 1675 forty years after the first colonists arrived, Maryland still had no large towns and only one village, St. Mary's, which had only a few hundred residents. Local government was conducted by county courts, which in turn were controlled by the richest planters. The county courts not only held trials, but also collected **taxes**, ran public services such as roads and ferries, issued tavern licenses, and held elections.

Tobacco culture along Maryland's riverfront plantations was similar to that of Virginia's [tobacco culture]. Soil lost its fertility after a few crops, and planters had to clear more fields or move on in search of more land. Planters relied mostly on the labor of indentured servants. Not until the later 1600s did they begin to import large numbers of African slaves.

As in Virginia, tobacco was used as money. In fact, tobacco was Maryland's currency only three years after the first English settlers landed. The planters overproduced tobacco in their quest for profits, causing its price to fall. High taxes imposed by the proprietor and English controls on the sale of tobacco to other nations also made it difficult for a small planter to make a living growing tobacco. By the late 1600s, former servants were no longer able to prosper from growing tobacco. Some became stuck in poverty and struggled to survive by working on other peoples' farms and plantations.

TAX: PAYMENT REQUIRED BY THE GOVERNMENT

An inland riverside port with its own customs house for receiving shipments from England. As settlers cleared more land, ports closed because creeks became silted up from soil washing into the waterways.

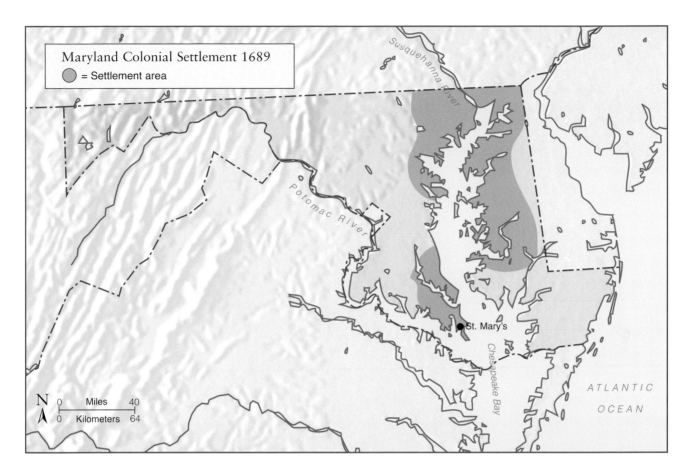

Maryland Colonial Settlement 1689

⬤ = Settlement area

Susquehanna River

Potomac River

Chesapeake Bay

● St. Mary's

ATLANTIC OCEAN

N

| 0 | Miles | 40 |
| 0 | Kilometers | 64 |

On this 1764 tobacco sales receipt, the buyer, a merchant in Scotland, lists the charges deducted from the payment for the tobacco, such as freight, taxes, and storage. When tobacco prices fell, the charges took a huge bite out of the planter's profits.

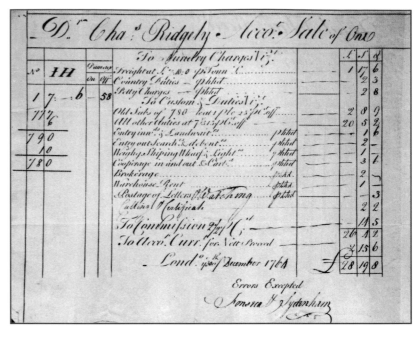

5:
MARYLAND'S BATTLES

BATTLES WITH THE NATIVE AMERICANS

The northern part of the Chesapeake Bay area had more beavers because it had more trees than Virginia's part of the bay. Englishmen from Virginia colony had been trading with the Maryland Native Americans for furs harvested from this area since the 1620s. In exchange for beaver **pelts,** the Native Americans wanted English cloth and metal tools. Lord Baltimore supported this trade. He did not grant much eastern shore land to English colonists because, as the Lord Proprietor, he made more money from taxes on the fur trade than he did on tobacco. Also, he thought the presence of friendly Native Americans on the eastern shore would be a buffer from hostile tribes to the north.

The most cooperative tribes on the eastern shore had their land protected by grants from the proprietor, for which they paid several beaver skins a year. Several fur traders requested and paid the rent on grants of Native American land just to keep tobacco planters from claiming the land and driving their Native American trading partners away. Still, English planters gradually occupied pieces of Native American land and thus reduced the native peoples' ability to freely move around in search of food. Maryland treaties guaranteed the Native Americans' traditional "hunting, fowling, crabbing, and fishing" rights, but in reality, English planters did not allow them to pursue these rights on their plantations. The Maryland government created reservations for the friendly Native Americans. The government intended these early reservations to protect the Native Americans' hold on their lands. Only later did the Maryland reservations become places of confinement.

In 1642 Maryland declared war on several groups of eastern shore Native Americans, including the Susquehannocks. The Susquehannocks received guns from the colonists of New Sweden, who had been living to the north in Delaware since 1638. The Swedish got along well with the Susquehannocks and wanted to keep trading with

PELT: SKIN AND FUR OF AN ANIMAL

Opposite: During Maryland's early colonial times, tobacco leaf was rolled into loose bundles for shipment. This was inefficient because it wasted valuable space aboard the ship. So tobacco began to be packed tightly into casks, barrels, and hogsheads. By the end of the 17th century, the tobacco was packed so tightly that a single hogshead of tobacco weighed nearly half a ton. It was hard to move such weights along America's primitive roads. Also, tobacco was delicate. If a hogshead was rolled over a land distance of more than 20 miles (32 kilometers), it suffered damage and loss of value.

them. They also wanted to keep the English colonists of Maryland from expanding into Delaware. The Susquehannocks used their Swedish-supplied guns to win a battle against the English in 1644.

Then in 1652 the Susquehannocks made peace with Maryland and gave the colony large tracts of land. The Susquehannocks had suffered huge losses in their war with the Iroquois and could no longer fight two wars at once. Both the Susquehannocks and the English considered the Iroquois people to be their enemies and feared Iroquois expansion into their territories. So the Susquehannocks and Maryland cooperated as allies to fight the Iroquois for the next twenty years.

Maryland did not treat its Susquehannock allies well. In 1674 the Maryland government ordered the Susquehannocks, who were weakened by decades of warfare, to move to a settlement on the banks of the Potomac River. The next year an argument between Native

Colonists living on the western frontier lived in fear of attack by Native Americans.

Americans and a Virginia landowner over ownership of some hogs ended in the murder of a Virginian and some twenty Native Americans. Fearing revenge, more than a thousand Virginia and Maryland **militia** surrounded the Susquehannock town. Militiamen murdered five Susquehannock chiefs whom they had invited to negotiate with them. The Susquehannocks fled their town for southern Virginia, and then took revenge by attacking and killing settlers on the **frontiers** of both colonies. They remained at war with the English and with other Maryland native peoples for another fifteen years, until they were reduced to scattered remnants. The Maryland assembly tried the militia commander for the murder of the five chiefs and found him guilty, but he was not punished.

Over the course of the colony's history, Native Americans lost about two thirds of their numbers to disease and to the periodic fights with the English. In the late 1600s and early 1700s, William Penn offered refuge in

FRONTIER: NEWEST PLACE OF SETTLEMENT, LOCATED THE FARTHEST AWAY FROM THE CENTER OF POPULATION

Nathaniel Bacon confronts the Governor Berkeley. Bacon's rebellion, a Virginia frontier uprising against the Native Americans in 1676, spilled over into the frontier region of Maryland. Angry and fearful frontier dwellers killed Native Americans at every opportunity, and ultimately destroyed them.

Oliver Cromwell (above) ruled England after the execution of King Charles I. When he died in 1658, his son could not hold onto power. Charles II returned to rule England in 1660.

his colony for some of the native peoples of Maryland. He allowed them to settle along the Susquehanna River, replacing the defeated Susquehannocks. Many Native Americans moved to the north and west of the Maryland colony by 1700. During the 1740s, most of the remaining eastern shore Native Americans found life in Maryland intolerable and went to live among the Iroquois in Pennsylvania and New York. The few that remained lived on small reservations under English control.

BATTLES FOR THE GOVERNMENT

Maryland had a legislature with an upper and a lower house, like the legislatures of the other English colonies. Maryland's charter called for a lower house, an assembly of free men to make laws or to approve laws made by the Proprietor. In fact, the proprietor made laws without assembly approval, and canceled most of the laws the assembly passed. The Proprietor also selected his family members and friends to serve in the upper house and to serve as Maryland's governor. Although the first assembly met in 1635, it was Lord Baltimore, the Proprietor, who held all the power.

Civil War broke out in England in 1642, making it difficult for Lord Baltimore, in England, to communicate with his brother, the governor in Maryland. The governor traveled to England to meet with his brother. While he was away, a Virginian took over some land in Maryland, and a Protestant tobacco trader from England seized Maryland's capital at St. Mary's. Governor Calvert returned from England in 1644, but because of the disorder he had to flee to Virginia. Until Calvert was able to re-take control of Maryland, the colony had no government for two years. Those years became known as "the plundering time," because, without a government, people stole and looted whatever they wanted.

To win more approval from the colonists, Lord Baltimore appointed a Protestant governor, and presented a new law calling for religious tolerance. But Lord Baltimore's vision of Catholics and Protestants living in harmony ended

up working against him. Several hundred Puritans, a dissenting group of Protestants, were expelled from Virginia and took refuge in Maryland. They soon outnumbered Maryland's Catholics and turned on the government.

The English Civil War ended in the execution of King Charles I in 1649, and the Puritan Oliver Cromwell ruled Parliament and through it, England. Charles I had been an Anglican, but, married to a Catholic, he tolerated some non-Anglicans. By 1654 Maryland's legislature had a majority of Puritans. They repealed the original Maryland law that guaranteed religious freedom and replaced it with a law forbidding both Catholicism and worship in the Church of England. Puritan radicals then drove priests from the colony, confiscated Catholic property, and executed four Catholics who took part in an attempt to recapture the capital. Calvert and his supporters did not give up. Lord Baltimore worked out a compromise with Oliver Cromwell that allowed the Calverts to regain control of Maryland's government in 1657.

A country church. The 1649 Act Concerning Religion stated: "Whatsoever person shall … call … any person … within this province an Heretic, Schismatic, Idolator, Puritan, Independent, Presbyterian, Popish Priest, Jesuit, Jesuited Papist, Lutheran, Calvinist, Anabaptist, Brownist, Antinomian, Barrowist, Roundhead, Separatist, or any other name or term in a reproachful manner relating to matters of religion, shall, for every such offense forfeit and lose the sum of ten shillings sterling." The new law promoting religious tolerance did not help Lord Baltimore keep control of his colony, but it did result in different Christian groups of Maryland building churches in which to worship as they chose.

Religious Freedom in the Colonies

Lord Baltimore s 1649 Act Concerning Religion outlawed religious intolerance toward different types of Christians. All of the known Christian sects Anglicans, Roman Catholics, Puritans, Quakers, Lutherans were to be protected in Maryland. They were forbidden to discriminate against one another, or even to speak badly about one another. The law extended only to people with some form of Christian belief. Non-Christians existed in a world beyond the protection of the law. Lord Baltimore hoped to protect his fellow Catholics when Protestants came to dominate Maryland, but his law did no good. Soon a group of Puritans threw Lord Baltimore and all other Catholics out of the Maryland government and began persecuting Catholics.

The first amendment to the United States Constitution says that Congress shall make no law respecting an establishment of religion. This means that no one religion can be the official religion of the United States. Before the founding of the United States, most of the colonies had an established church, or official religion, supported by taxes collected from all citizens. Only Rhode Island, Delaware, and Pennsylvania did not.

Puritan colonists came to New England in search of freedom to practice their form of Christianity, but they did not grant that freedom to other Christians. Instead, most of the Puritan New England colonies made their own church the official one, and had Quakers executed for their faith. Quakers suffered persecution everywhere except Pennsylvania.

The middle and southern colonies established the Church of England as their official church. In the end, the Protestant majority forced Maryland s proprietors to give up Catholicism and establish the Church of England as the official church of Maryland.

This building housed the government of colonial Maryland for several years while it was still at St. Mary's.

Maryland's Lord Proprietor then granted land to Catholic churches, In addition, Catholics received most high political offices. When the government also imposed high taxes without the approval of the elected assembly, Marylanders became deeply upset. However, Lord Baltimore refused to listen to any complaints, and appointed another Catholic governor. Yet Protestants made up 80 percent of Maryland's population. This resentful majority waited for their chance.

After the Protestant King William and Queen Mary took the English throne from the Catholic King James II in 1689, Maryland's governor canceled the meeting of the assembly. Protestant rebels then marched on St. Mary's and overthrew the Calverts' **proprietary** government. Maryland became a Protestant royal colony, which it

PROPRIETARY: PRIVATELY OWNED

King James II ruled England for barely three years, from 1685 to 1688. He was a Catholic, which many English people found objectionable, and he tried to bypass Parliament in making laws. Worse, he raised taxes throughout England's empire and tried to increase royal authority over the colonies. He banned the colonial legislatures and appointed a dictator, Sir Edmund Andros, over all of the New England colonies, plus New York and New Jersey. Andros began to collect rents from land that colonists already owned. Discontented Protestants in England wrote to James' nephew, William, in the Netherlands. William landed in England with an army, and James fled to France, leaving the throne to William and his wife, Mary.

QUAKERS: MEMBERS OF THE SOCIETY OF FRIENDS, A CHRISTIAN GROUP FOUNDED IN ENGLAND AROUND 1650

remained for nearly 25 years. King William appointed a Protestant officer, Lionel Copley, as royal governor of Maryland. The Lord Proprietor was still allowed to control the distribution of any available land in Maryland, but he could no longer govern the colony. The new government barred Catholics and **Quakers** from holding any political office. In 1692 the Protestant government declared that the Church of England was the official established church of the colony. In 1694 the capital was moved from Catholic-dominated St. Mary's to Protestant-controlled Annapolis, where it remained permanently.

Benedict Calvert, the fourth Lord Baltimore, renounced Catholicism and joined the Church of England. He then asked King George I to restore his proprietorship of Maryland. The King granted his request in 1715. The laws of Maryland were brought into line with English law, and from that time on, the colony's government remained essentially unchanged. The days of Maryland as a Catholic haven passed into history.

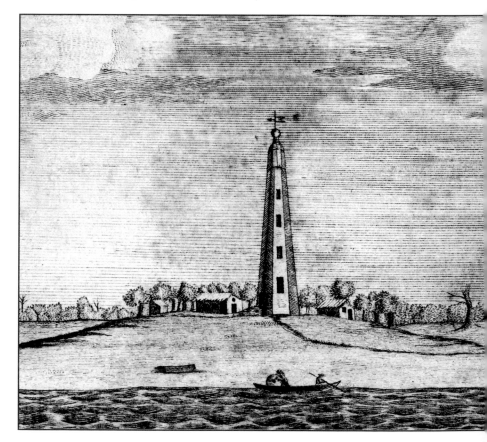

BATTLES FOR THE BORDERLANDS

The Lords of Maryland competed for land with the other European colonies as well as with Native Americans. They disputed Maryland's borders with Virginia, Delaware, and Pennsylvania. Having overcome Virginia's opposition to Maryland's very existence, on arrival there the settlers ejected a Virginian, William Claiborne, from an island he claimed in the Chesapeake Bay. Claiborne returned during the "plundering time" ten years later to try to reclaim the island, only to be expelled again when the Calvert family regained control of Maryland.

The Lords Baltimore believed that their charter also gave them control of the land around the Delaware Bay. Delaware came under Dutch control, for the second time in its history, in 1673. Lord Baltimore used this as an excuse to send a troop of horsemen to claim land around Delaware Bay, near present-day Lewes, for England. On Christmas Eve, 1673, the Maryland troops burned the

Maryland's proprietors claimed that their colony included Cape Henlopen, on the western side of Delaware Bay. Cape Henlopen now lies in Delaware.

entire settlement, preventing the inhabitants—Dutch, Swedish, and English—from saving any of their possessions. The attackers took all boats, horses, guns, and food, and left the villagers stranded in the winter weather. The local Native Americans kindly took them in. One survivor reported that "the Indians that lived here about wept when they saw the spoil that the inhabitants had suffered by their own native countrymen."

Mapmakers friendly with the Calvert family cleverly moved the northern border of Maryland a bit farther north when they drew a new map. Once William Penn became proprietor of a colony in Pennsylvania in 1681, the two colonies argued over their long common border. In 1684 Penn returned to England to argue for his claim to the border lands. Only the hiring of the English surveyors Charles Mason and Jeremiah Dixon in 1763 firmly established Maryland's northern border with Pennsylvania.

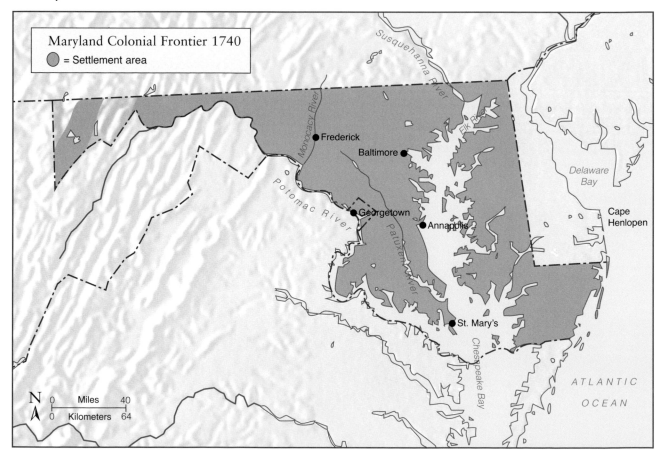

6.
THE GROWTH OF MARYLAND

During the 1700s settlers moved inland, crossed the fall line, and entered the Piedmont. There they found soils that could grow tobacco, wheat, and corn. The settlers had to move this produce overland or in small boats to the fall line in order to load them aboard oceangoing vessels that carried their goods to Europe. Similarly, imports, all the manufactured goods and luxury items made in Europe, had to be unloaded below the fall line and reloaded for overland transportation. Consequently, warehouses to store goods, taverns to feed and house people, and all sorts of related structures sprung up near the fall line of major rivers. Over time, these places grew into riverfront towns such as Baltimore, Upper Marlboro, and Georgetown.

A colonial riverfront settlement in northeastern Maryland, near the Pennsylvania border

Main picture: Colonial shipbuilders

Inset: Baltimore in 1752

Increasing population and increasing wealth also caused Annapolis to blossom. Since Annapolis was both the colony's capital and a port on a navigable river, it grew particularly rapidly. Annapolis had many shipyards where skilled carpenters, sailmakers, and ship suppliers worked.

By about 1720 small farmers began to settle the mountainous back country on the western frontier. Many Quakers, Germans, and Scots traveled south from Pennsylvania and settled in western Maryland. Some of them continued through the rugged mountains of western Maryland to Virginia's Shenandoah Valley.

Frederick became the principal town of western Maryland. In addition to the county courthouse, Frederick boasted numerous shops and warehouses, neat brick,

Inset: Annapolis has been the capital of Maryland since 1694. The statehouse built in 1772 is still in use.

After the earliest days when survival was a struggle, colonists enjoyed more land with higher fertility and more plentiful food than in England.

stone, and wood houses, and places of worship for the different Christian groups. **Lutheran** and German Reformed churches for the German settlers shared the town with Quaker meeting houses and an Anglican (Church of England) church. In contrast to the tobacco plantations worked by slaves in the east, western

Marylanders grew wheat, corn, and other grains without slave labor. They grew enough extra crops to trade for English goods. During the 1700s, Maryland also began producing iron. Iron forges sprang up rapidly throughout the colony, and by the 1750s the colony was exporting thousands of tons to England each year.

The People of Maryland Colony

Maryland's population grew slowly, reaching about 13,000 in 1675, more than 40 years after the first English settlers arrived. Of these 13,000, only about 1,200 were African slaves. Twenty-five years later, by 1700, the colonial population had grown to about 32,000. Of this number, 3,000 were Africans. By 1720, the population had surpassed 60,000, and one in five was black.

Between 1720 and 1760, Maryland's population grew from 60,000 to 160,000. Of the total, about 49,000 were black and all but 1,000 of them were slaves. By this time, the adult population was evenly split between men and women. Nearly a half of the total population was under the age of 15. Of the European origin population (about 111,000), 5,000 were indentured servants, and about 1,500 were transported convicts.

By the time of the Revolution, 65% of the European origin colonists in Maryland were English, 12% German, and 7% Scottish.

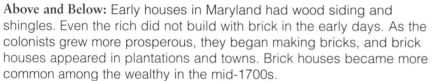

Above and Below: Early houses in Maryland had wood siding and shingles. Even the rich did not build with brick in the early days. As the colonists grew more prosperous, they began making bricks, and brick houses appeared in plantations and towns. Brick houses became more common among the wealthy in the mid-1700s.

Left: The class system of England survived in America, in spite of the fact that colonists were able to change their social status through hard work. Even people who had simple houses bought fine furnishings as soon as they could afford them. In 1744 a wealthy Maryland man complained that common people should be satisfied with wooden plates and spoons, and that fine goods should only be for the rich. Around that time, a tenant farmer, who owned no land, had an average of 26 pounds [English money] worth of possessions to his name. A man with a small farm had land and goods worth an average of 117 pounds, while a slave-owning planter had about 600 pounds worth of land, goods, and slaves. Colonists valued their possessions—including weapons, pots, tools, clothing, and mattresses—so much that they put them in their wills.

Below: A slave dwelling, with the plantation house in the background. In 1650 there were only about 300 African slaves in the Chesapeake Bay region. Fifty years later there were 3,000. After the price of tobacco crashed in the 1660s, it became more difficult for freed servants to prosper. As a result fewer English people wanted to come to the colonies as servants. By 1700 very few Maryland planters still had indentured servants, and most had switched to slaves.

Right: One of colonial Maryland's oldest plantation houses, built near St. Mary's around 1650. The largest plantations, such as those owned by Daniel Dulany and Charles Carroll, had 20,000 to 40,000 acres. In the early 1700s, more than half the men in Maryland did not own any land.

7.
MARYLAND IN THE FRENCH AND INDIAN WAR

Maryland played only a minor role in the French and Indian War (1754–1763), during which Britain and France fought one another for control of Canada and the land to the west of the Allegheny Mountains. Early in the war, Native Americans began raiding settlements on the western frontier, killing settlers or driving them from their homes. The planters living safely in the eastern part of the colony controlled the Maryland assembly. They had no interest in spending Maryland's money to defend the frontier. They also expected that Pennsylvania and Virginia would defend Maryland's comparatively small western border, which was sandwiched between the longer frontiers of the two bordering colonies.

In 1755 Great Britain sent more than 1,000 soldiers to North America under the command of General Edward Braddock. They landed in Virginia, where they were joined by George Washington and about 450 Virginia and Maryland soldiers. Braddock, Washington, and their men marched straight across Virginia to fight the French in Pennsylvania. On the way, they stopped at Fort Cumberland, in far western Maryland. The force left Fort Cumberland in June 1755 and began a month-long march to re-take Fort Duquesne, in western Pennsylvania, from the French. The march ended in a crushing British loss when French and Native American fighters ambushed the army on July 9. This loss became known as Braddock's Defeat. Braddock's Defeat occurred close enough to Maryland to make the legislators nervous, and they reluctantly passed a tax to pay for troops.

Annapolis, as the capital, was the center of social and cultural life. Its citizens could afford to ignore the war on the frontier. Each year the governor threw a party on the Lord Proprietor's birthday, serving drinks to everyone. Gentlemen's social clubs formed, where men met to drink and discuss politics and books. One such club, the Tuesday Club, met in Annapolis from 1744 to 1756. A member drew this picture of one of the club's early meetings.

As the French and Indian War continued, Maryland contributed very little to the war effort. The legislators simply did not see it as their war, and did not recognize the right of Britain to insist on Maryland's help as one of its colonies. They flatly refused the orders of the British commander-in-chief to send Maryland militia to **garrison** Fort Cumberland, or to pay for supplies. They argued that Fort Cumberland, technically in Maryland, existed mainly to protect the Virginia frontier, and that Virginia should pay to man and supply it. By 1757 Maryland had fewer than 150 armed men defending the frontier or helping the British fight the war. No other colony stood in such open defiance to royal authority during this war.

After the French and British signed a peace treaty in 1763, several Native American groups joined forces against the British and raided frontier settlements in the western parts of Pennsylvania, Maryland, and Virginia. This period was known as Pontiac's Rebellion. The western settlers asked the Maryland government for help in defending the frontier, but once again, the legislators took no action.

GARRISON: TO SUPPLY TROOPS TO A MILITARY POST OR FORT

Although Fort Cumberland lay within Maryland's borders, the Maryland government did not send soldiers to protect it. They reasoned that Virginia and Pennsylvania had longer frontiers and more settlers at risk from Native American attack, and therefore should be responsible for operating the fort.

8.
REBELLION

The Lords Baltimore had struggled to control the government of their colony almost since its beginning. Protestants, elected assemblymen, and rivals from outside the colony had challenged the Calvert family's authority at every opportunity. The proprietors had always supported the **crown** and were seen as favorites of England's royalty. Maryland's assembly had a long history of refusing to cooperate with the governor, the proprietor, or the crown.

The French and Indian War had been expensive for Great Britain, so Parliament imposed new taxes on the colonies to help pay for the war. The first new tax law, the Sugar **Act** of 1764, did not upset many people in Maryland, because they were not heavily trading in the taxed products. However, the

Stamp Act of 1765—which required colonists to pay to have most business and legal documents, as well as newspapers, stamped—upset Marylanders along with the rest of colonial **America**. Maryland was suffering from a depression in tobacco prices at the time the Stamp Act passed. Money was scarce and people felt unable to bear the burden of a new tax.

When an Annapolis merchant, Zachariah Hood, asked for and received the job of selling the tax stamps, demonstrations and riots broke out. Mobs destroyed Hood's warehouse and burned him in effigy. Fearing for his life, he fled Maryland. For once, the assembly and the governor agreed. The governor and proprietor resented the Stamp Act because it overrode their own authority

Opposite, Top: A British tax stamp. The Stamp Act required colonists to pay for the privilege of having all their documents stamped.

Opposite, Bottom: People gathered throughout the colonies to protest taxes imposed by authorities living on the far side of the ocean.

Published in Annapolis beginning in 1727, the Maryland Gazette printed many letters protesting the Stamp Act, and then ceased publication before the Stamp Act took effect, rather than pay the tax.

ACT: LAW; SO CALLED BECAUSE IT IS MADE BY AN ACT OF GOVERNMENT

CROWN: THE BRITISH KING OR QUEEN

AMERICA: LAND THAT CONTAINS THE CONTINENTS OF NORTH AMERICA AND SOUTH AMERICA

Theater became popular in Annapolis beginning arbout 1752. A theater was built in 1772. This painting shows an actress in a 1770 play presented in Annapolis

over the colony. Maryland's governor allowed the assembly to meet early, so that it could send delegates to New York for the Stamp Act Congress, organized to protest the Act. The assembly selected the delegates and passed resolutions declaring that only Maryland had the right to impose taxes on its people. In a rare display of unity, the upper house approved the lower house's actions, and the governor signed the resolutions immediately.

Maryland at first ceased all official business rather than use the hated stamps. Groups calling themselves the Sons of Liberty formed throughout the colonies to resist the Stamp Act. Sons of Liberty in Baltimore and the counties demanded that business be conducted without the stamps, in open defiance of the act. They also wrote to groups in the other colonies to coordinate their efforts. The Sons of Liberty convinced the Maryland courts and government offices to reopen without obeying the Stamp Act. A few days later, the news arrived that Parliament had repealed the act.

The widespread unpopularity of the Stamp Act had swayed Parliament this time. Still, King George III insisted that Great Britain's parliament had the right to make laws for the colonies and collect taxes. Parliament passed a new set of tax laws in 1767. Maryland merchants joined other

Not until 1748 did Maryland pass a law requiring all tobacco to be inspected. Virginia had long required inspections, so their tobacco gained a reputation for better quality than Maryland's product. Here, slaves load tobacco at a colonial dock.

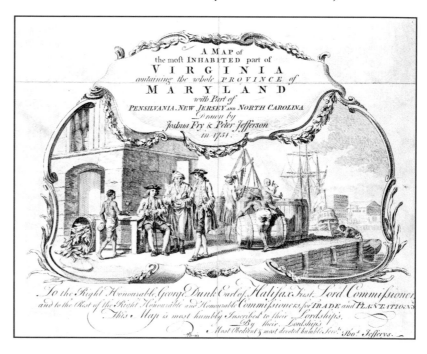

> BOYCOTT: AN AGREEMENT TO REFUSE TO BUY FROM OR SELL TO CERTAIN BUSINESSES

American merchants in **boycotting** English merchandise rather than paying taxes on it. Most of the boycott's organizers in Maryland were members of the legislature. Local committees formed to enforce the **boycott** and convince—or frequently threaten—merchants to participate. The boycott convinced the British to repeal most taxes by 1770, except for the tax on tea.

Parliament passed a new law in 1773, which gave one British tea merchant a monopoly on tea sales in the colonies. This enraged the colonists and they once again organized protests. The Sons of Liberty made plans to disrupt tea shipments. The first and most famous tea protest was the Boston Tea Party of December 1773. Patriots disguised as Native Americans boarded a trading ship and dumped many cases of tea into Boston Harbor. Parliament responded with the Boston Port Act, which punished Boston by shutting down its port.

The Boston Port Act did not stop other colonists from having their own "tea parties." Citizens of a small town on the Chester River in Maryland dumped tea from a ship in May 1774. Six months later, the much more destructive Annapolis Tea Party occurred. The local committee forced a merchant to burn his own ship, which carried a ton of tea, along with other trade goods. Maryland patriots

The fireplace at a colonial customs house in eastern Maryland. Ships stopped at customs houses for inspection by tax collectors.

EPILOGUE

Below: In 1783 George Washington went to Annapolis to resign as commander-in-chief of the Continental Army. The victorious general was a hero to the new nation and could have taken over the government and become very powerful. Instead he retired to his plantation and left all authority in the hands of the congress.

After the end of the Revolution, Annapolis became the temporary capital of the new United States. There, in Maryland's State House, General George Washington resigned his commission as commander-in-chief of the Continental Army and resumed his life as a civilian. Also in Annapolis, the Congress approved the 1783 Treaty of Paris, which ended the Revolutionary War.

In 1788 Maryland became the seventh state to ratify the U.S. Constitution and join the United States. In 1791 Maryland gave up a piece of land for the new national capital, which became the District of Columbia.

Where the Appalachian Mountains cross Maryland, the forests remain nearly unchanged. The Cheseapeake Bay, however, has seen a lot of change brought about by storm-driven saltwater. The island on which the first colonists landed is barely a tenth of what its size was in 1634. Silt and pollution have greatly reduced the numbers of oysters and crabs that once existed in abundance to feed Native Americans and colonists alike.

More than five million people live in Maryland today. About one quarter of the state's population is black. Only a few thousand people of Native American ancestry live scattered throughout Maryland. A large part of Maryland's population now lives around the nation's capital, where many work for the government.

Annapolis, Maryland's capital since 1694, has a historic district with several buildings from the colonial era still in use. St. Mary's, Maryland colony's first settlement and capital, lost much of its population when the capital was moved to Annapolis. It is now a historical site that includes replicas of the Dove, the first state house, village buildings, and a tobacco plantation.

Below Right: A farmer hauls tobacco in St. Mary's County in the early 20th century. Farmers still grow tobacco in southern Maryland.

DATELINE

JUNE 20, 1632: Lord Baltimore receives a grant of land with a charter to found a colony in America.

NOVEMBER 22, 1633: Two ships, the *Ark* and the *Dove*, carrying the first Maryland colonists, set sail from England.

MARCH 1634: The *Ark* and the *Dove* reach Maryland.

1642: Maryland declares war on the Susquehannocks.

1644–1646: "the plundering time." Maryland's government is overthrown by English outlaws while Governor Calvert is in England.

1649: Maryland passes the Act Concerning Religion, to promote religious tolerance.

1652: Maryland signs a peace treaty with the Susquehannocks.

1654: A Puritan majority takes over Maryland and drives the Calvert family from the government.

1657: Lord Baltimore regains control of Maryland.

1675: The Susquehannocks resume their war with the English settlers of Maryland and carry it on until they are destroyed permanently as a nation.

1681: William Penn receives a charter to found a colony to the north of Maryland, beginning an argument over the Pennsylvania-Maryland border that will not end until 1763.

1689: Protestants overthrow the Calverts and Maryland becomes a royal colony.

1694: The capital of Maryland is moved from St. Mary's to Annapolis, where it remains.

1715: The fourth Lord Baltimore regains control of Maryland colony.

1729: The city of Baltimore is founded.

JUNE 1755: An army led by General Braddock marches from Fort Cumberland, Maryland, in a failed attempt to capture Fort Duquesne from the French.

1765: Maryland rioters drive the stamp tax collector from the colony.

1774: Maryland patriots destroy two tea shipments.

NOVEMBER 11, 1776: Maryland approves a constitution and becomes an independent state.

GLOSSARY

ACT: law; so called because it is made by an act of government

AMERICA: land that contains the continents of North America and South America

ANGLICAN: Church of England, a Protestant church and the state church of England

BOYCOTT: agreement to refuse to buy from or sell to certain businesses

CATHOLIC: Roman Catholic; the oldest Christian church organization, governed by a hierarchy based in Rome and led by the pope.

CHARTER: document containing the rules for running an organization

COLONY: land owned and controlled by a distant nation; a colonist is a permanent settler of a colony

CROWN: king or queen

FALL LINE: point at which a river flows from high ground toward sea level

FRONTIER: newest place of settlement, located the farthest away from the center of population

GARRISON: to supply troops to a military post or fort

HOGSHEAD: large barrel used to transport tobacco

INDENTURE: agreement to work for someone for a certain number of years, in exchange for food, a place to sleep, and payment of one's passage across the Atlantic to the colonies

INDIANS: name given to all Native Americans at the time Europeans first came to America, because it was believed that America was actually a close neighbor of India

INQUISITION: state-sponsored persecution of non-Catholics in Spain and Portugal, noted for the use of torture

JESUIT: member of the Society of Jesus, a men's religious order founded in 1540. Jesuits have always been very active as missionaries around the world.

LUTHERAN: form of Protestantism based on the ideas of Martin Luther, a 16th century German monk who questioned Catholicism

MILITIA: group of citizens not normally part of the army who join together to defend their land in an emergency

NEW WORLD: western hemisphere of the earth, including North America, Central America, and South America; so called because the people of the Old World, in the east, did not know about the existence of the Americas until the 1400s

NOBILITY: members of English high social class just below royalty, possessing titles or ranks that were either inherited or given by the king or queen

PARLIAMENT: legislature of Great Britain

PELT: skin and fur of an animal

PERSECUTE: to punish people because of their beliefs, religion, or race

PILGRIMS: Puritans that separated from the Church of England instead of trying to change it from within

PLANTER: owner of a plantation, or large farm

POUND: currency, or form of money, used by the British

PROPRIETARY: privately owned

PROTESTANT: any Christian church that has broken from away from Roman Catholic or Eastern Orthodox control

PURITANS: Protestants who wanted the Church of England to practice a more "pure" form of Christianity

QUAKERS: members of the Society of Friends, a Christian group founded in England around 1650

STOCKADE: series of wooden posts set into the ground, forming a high wall to protect a settlement

TAX: payment required by the government

FURTHER READING

Collier, Christopher and James Lincoln Collier. *The French and Indian War, 1660–1763.* Tarrytown, N.Y.: Marshall Cavendish, 1998.

Smith, Carter, ed. *Daily Life: A Source Book on Colonial America.* Brookfield, Conn.: Millbrook Press, 1991.

Smith, Carter, ed. *The Revolutionary War: A Source Book on Colonial America.* Brookfield, Conn.: Millbrook Press, 1991.

Tunis, Edwin. *Colonial Living.* Baltimore: Johns Hopkins University Press, 1999.

WEBSITES

www.americaslibrary.gov
Select "Jump back in time" for links to history activities.

http://www.fortedwards.org/cwffa/cwffhome.htm
Explore frontier forts involved in the French and Indian War.

http://www.thinkquest.org/library/JR-index.html
Look up links to numerous student-designed sites about American colonial history.

BIBLIOGRAPHY

Duke, Maurice. *Chesapeake Bay Voices: Narratives from Four Centuries.* Richmond, Va.: Dietz Press, 1993.

The American Heritage History of the Thirteen Colonies. American Heritage Publishing Co., 1967.

Hawke, David Freeman. *Everyday Life in Early America.* New York: Harper & Row, 1988.

Middleton, Arthur Pierce. *Tobacco Coast: A Maritime History of Chesapeake Bay in the Colonial Era.* Newport News, Va.: Mariners' Museum, 1953.

Middleton, Richard. *Colonial America: A History, 1607–1760.* Cambridge, Mass.: Blackwell, 1992.

Quinn, David B., ed. *Early Maryland in a Wider World.* Detroit: Wayne State University Press, 1982.

Taylor, Alan. *American Colonies.* New York: Viking, 2001.

INDEX